# Iceland and the Icelanders

*by*

## Helgi P. Briem

*Color Photography by*

### Vigfús Sigurgeirsson

*Published by*

**JOHN FRANCIS McKENNA COMPANY**
MAPLEWOOD, NEW JERSEY

FIRST EDITION

This book is manufactured under wartime conditions in conformity
with government regulations controlling the use of paper
and other materials.

*View of Reykjavik*

# ICELAND

Iceland is one of the great stepping stones between America and Europe. It is disputed whether it belongs to the Western or Eastern Hemisphere. Geographically it is closer to the great land-masses of the American continent than to Europe. It would therefore be natural to regard it as the easternmost outpost of America.

The people of Iceland and its culture are, however, completely European. Of the many nations that inhabited America before white men ever saw it, those living in the northernmost parts are called Eskimos. As far as we know they have never penetrated to Iceland. While they roamed

*A fishing boat at Hornafjordur*

over the islands of North America in skin-covered boats, the Scandinavians called Vikings roamed over the Islands of Northern Europe in wooden boats.

The Vikings seem to have been sailors of genius and of great courage. Without compass and without maps they sailed enormous distances never sighting land. They developed a fine sense of landscape and found descriptive names that fitted the place so well that still to-day we can identify their sailing routes with the help of the names which have survived in Icelandic writings.

When the Vikings discovered the island about 870 A.D. they gave it several names. The name that survived was Iceland. Everybody coming

*Wintersports*

from Europe sees as the first sign of land the gleaming ice domes resting on the high Icelandic mountains. Down the valleys glaciers descend like frozen waterfalls. This was a sight undreamt of before. No sailor from Europe had seen such gigantic snow-covered mountains, for they do not exist there in view from the sea.

The country was called Iceland. But about 975 A.D. Icelanders sailed to explore another country to the north and west of Iceland. They found a huge island. But whereas Iceland has individual mountain systems covered with ice, the entire interior of this new country was covered with an ice dome for hundreds of miles. Here the name Iceland would have been appropriate. But the name that survived is Greenland.

*A winter panorama*

That was so striking that it has been used ever since. The Icelanders, who always liked their joke, gave Erik, the discoverer of Greenland, the surname: the Red. One wonders whether they were trying to top the name of Greenland or whether he got it from describing the color of the Redskins to his unbelieving audience.

Now everybody is familiar with the fact that it gets colder the higher one gets, for even at the Equator the mountains are snow covered if they are high enough. Iceland means the land where the mountains are covered with ice.

As a matter of fact the climate of Iceland is not very cold. In Reykjavik the coldest month is January. The mean temperature for that

*The vicarage Grund at Eyjafjordur*

month is 1 degree above freezing, or about 33° F. In New York it is 31.3 or 1.7 degrees colder on the average. In Albany, New York, it is 23.3° F, in Chicago it is 25.6° F. This is an average, so it does not show the extremes, but in America they are much greater than in Iceland. Nearly every winter New Yorkers experience much severer frosts than the people of Reykjavik.

It is never very cold nor very hot. The summers are cool with a mean temperature of about 50° F. and the heat seldom rising above 70° F. There are no great extremes in the Icelandic climate. It is often windy there but the wind rarely rises to great strength. It is very changeable and one can often get a good sample of everything the weather man has to

*A lavastream from Snaefellsjokull*

offer within 24 hours. It rains a great deal, and the snow that falls in the winter seldom lies for a long time. A good raincoat is more necessary than a thick overcoat, and furs have never been worn there until very recently and then only by the ladies. It is an invigorating climate that suits some people, and you either love it or loath it.

To understand the Icelandic landscape one must mention a few geological facts. Iceland is very volcanic. It is one of the few places where one can still see the world in the making. Its volcanoes still eject glowing lava. Its glaciers still push forward millions of tons of stones and dirt, scooping out great valleys in the process.

*View of the South coast*

Iceland is situated on a great submarine ridge stretching from Great Britain to America. Some think this is a mountain chain of a sunken continent. During the last Glacial Age Iceland seems to have carried a gigantic load of ice and when the ice receded, probably some seven to nine thousand years ago much of the present lowlands were submerged. For thousands of years the waves battered against the rocky shore of Iceland, and this explains the nearly perpendicular fall of the mountains facing the sea, undercut by waves of a sea seldom quiet.

The work of the waves was made easier by the fact that Iceland is built up of layer upon layer of basalt, each layer representing a lava flood. In Western Iceland we can count up to 80 layers varying in thickness

*Kirkjufell at Grundarfjordur*

from 2 inches to 250 feet. Each layer is somewhat loosely attached to the layer beneath. Its surface has perhaps been covered by scoriae and ashes, soil and woods. This means than the Icelandic mountains are not very resistant to the forces of erosion, wind, frost, and water, and Iceland has certainly been much bigger in the past.

These sedimentary beds between the basalt layers are the archives of our geological history. At Brjanslaekur in North Western Iceland we find petrified woods and leaves easily identifiable. The leaves have collected in great masses in a still lake surrounded by woods of maple and sequoia, oak and beech, birch and elm, tulip tree and walnut tree and many others.

*The Godalands glacier*

To the east of Brjanslaekur in Steingrimsfjordur there is a petrified wood of sequoia. It has obviously been showered by an eruption of hot pumice-stone which probably killed it.

Later this old surface has been covered by lavafloods one on top of the other, at least to a thickness of twelve to fourteen thousand feet. Mountains of that height would of course be covered by glaciers and in between the lava layers are also found moraines, i.e. loose material ground by glaciers to clay, sand or loose rounded stones as are so very common in North America, for instance in Long Island.

When these glaciers receded they left some parts of the country very like what it is now. The North Western peninsula of Iceland is one of the

*Fnjoskadalur with brush land*

most illuminating examples of recent glacial action to be found in the
world. In a small area gigantic glaciers have cut up its plateau into fjords
until hardly any plateau is left. The small glacier that has scooped out
Vatnsfjordur and opened the deposits of Brjanslaekur to our view, has
dug out the fjord to a depth of 540 feet and carried deposits to the mouth
of the fjord so that it is only 30-50 feet deep. But Isafjordur is entered
through a royal portal over ten miles wide, flanked by precipitous mountains 1500-2000 feet high, sculptured out by the main ice-stream.

The ice-eroded landscapes of Iceland are filled with a strange majesty.
They are formed of vertical or slightly inclined layers of basalt, usually
rather dark in colour, giving it poise and gravity. The ice has undercut

*Ketillaugarfjall in Hornafjordur*

the mountain sides leaving them very steep. Between the valleys are great ridges and though these are often flat topped, to the eyes of the onlooker they look like fantastic peaks. This landscape is somewhat somber, but relieved by brooks that fall in merry little waterfalls forming silver incrustations in the flanks of the mountains.

Owing to the young formations in Iceland these brooks have not had time to unite and build up great drainage areas and the mountains are therefore streaked with small gullies at regular intervals. But even the smallest brook loosens a considerable amount of rock in the course of time. This loose material builds up as a cone at the mountain side, hiding its foot and forming a grassy slope that further relieves its somber flank.

*The farm at Thingvellir*

Some people find this pattern of sharp cones reflected in the oldfashioned farm buildings of Iceland.

In this landscape we also find the ruins of enormous old volcanoes. The core of a volcano is usually of a more resistant nature than the loose material flung out. As an example of these ruins can be mentioned Baula in Borgarfjordur. It has been worn by wind and weather until it is now a triangular pyramid so steep that no snow can settle there to form a glacier. It is of a rock of light colour called liparite, and one must assume that the volcano has at some time ejected liparite. From the size of the neck it must once have formed a mountain structure of great size. But no remnants have been found of the superstructure, indicating the gigantic

*The Kristnes farm at Eyjafjordur*

carrying power of the glaciers of the Glacial Age, which have not left anything of the volcano but the neck.

If it is right that high mountains rested on a basaltic structure which from present remnants we can estimate to be 12-14,000 feet, we can dimly perceive that even without a subsidence the Icelandic mountains have been in the same class as the loftiest mountains we now know.

Perhaps the glaciers and the waves between them would have broken Iceland down to a group of small islands if it had not been for an extremely vigorous volcanic activity. About one-eighth of Iceland is now covered with lava streams that have flowed since the glaciation, but great areas are covered by tuff which in many cases originates from vol-

*Akureyri seen across the fjord*

canic ashes and we do not know the age of this.

We know of about 150 volcanoes that have been active since the glaciation. Some of these have built up quite impressive cones, among them Oraefajokull, the highest mountain in Iceland (6950 feet), in the top of which there is a crater filled with ice and water forming an almost circular plain 3 miles in diameter.

The best known volcano is Hekla (4746 feet). Annals mention 22 eruptions of this volcano since 1104 A.D., and some of these eruptions have been very destructive. Its notoriety is, however, due to the fact that the clergy of the Middle Ages found it convenient to say that Hekla was the entrance to that hot Inferno in which some sinners did not properly

*Helgafell, a small volcano at Vestmannaeyjar*

believe. Still to-day several peoples in Europe consign to Hekla those whom they would like to get rid of and expect would go in vain to the Pearly Gates.

There are many lava domes, peculiar volcanic formations, that probably were formed by one single eruption. Among these can be mentioned Skjaldbreidur, which has a nearly perfectly even slope on all sides. It is over 3000 feet high and has a diameter of about 7 miles.

The eruption of the Laki craters in 1783 ranks as one of the greatest eruptions in historical times, if not the greatest. This was a fissure eruption where a crack in the earth's surface ejected enormous masses of lava. The fissure is about 20 miles long and whereas in the beginning of the eruption the lava flowed directly from the fissure, towards the end, it formed about a hundred small cones each with a crater. In about 5 months there were ejected what has been estimated to be 400 billion cubic feet of lava, but in addition another 100 billion cubic feet must be added for ashes and small matter some of which was thrown up into the stratosphere. This would be more than the cubic content of the highest mountain in Europe: Mont Blanc.

The effect of this eruption was felt all over the world, and seen in the brilliant sunsets caused by the ashes in the stratosphere.

The lava that streams from a volcano is red hot and over 850 centigrades. It usually follows the waterways and often has filled up great canyons leaving the rivers to dig a new course. Often great lakes at the edges of the lava streams are dammed up, as can be seen in the lakes of the Sog, the outlet of Thingvallavatn. One such canyon of great beauty is the Asbyrgi which Jokulsa in Axarfjordur had begun to dig but the river later was pushed further east by a lava stream and has since dug a beautiful canyon. Where the river falls down into the canyon it forms one of the most powerful waterfalls in Europe: Dettifoss.

Of the recent lava fields many are buried in soil and overgrown with grass and heather, birch and willow. These are the oldest. The "middle aged" are being covered by moss, while the newest are like slag just come from the oven, for most of the lava streams are covered with loose slag. The only adequate description of a recent lava field is to compare it with the sea whipped by a hurricane and petrified during one instant of its wildest movement.

The snow line in Iceland is at about 3000 feet. This means that snow

*A glacier calving into an inland lake in the highlands*

that falls on mountains above that height will not melt completely in the summer. The remnant covers the mountain and forms an icecap that would grow to heaven if it did not find an outlet. The ice glides like a thick liquid off the mountain and down to warmer regions where it melts. When it is on the move it is called a glacier.

Iceland has a great mountain system in the southeast coast about which we know very little, for it is covered with a thick ice-cap, called Vatnajokull. From the icecap fall a number of glaciers, each of which has a name. The extent of this ice covered area is about 3300 square miles. In it we know there are hot springs and volcanoes. Some valleys have been wooded recently for the glaciers have pushed out tree trunks and peat.

There are a number of other ice caps each of which is a drainage center. In all directions from them run brooks that join into great rivers. Owing to the mountainous landscape they have a swift current and carry a great load of silt, which gives them a colour that can change from milky white to chocolate brown. As soon as they slow down, they drop the silt which forms a barrier and forces the river to seek another outlet. These glacier-rivers are therefore constantly changing and throw their water from one side of the valleys to the other, forming one of the chief barriers to travel in Iceland. Besides they form at the bottom of the valley a black desolation of stones, a melancholy, but rather magnificent desert. It is very difficult to bridge them, for they change from hour to hour according to the melting of the glaciers that feed them. When they freeze, they freeze from the bottom which means that though they form a levee the ice on the stones at the bottom lifts them over the levee to find a new course.

Besides the glacier-rivers we have many rivers of clear water which originate in springs. These are quite different in behavior and follow a regular course with grassgrown banks, like the rivers elsewhere. Their origin is interesting. Due to the porosity of the lava in the ground the water sinks in and runs subterraneously for long distances. On the big Reykjanesskagi to the south of Reykjavik there is not a single river visible, as all the drainage is subterraneous. It has been mentioned above that the lava streams follow the river courses. The water, however, seeks its old course and seeps through the lava. The lava acts as a gigantic water filter and the rivers emerge purified and sparkling as the brooks of Paradise.

*The twisting course of glacier rivers*

Often rivers undercut the edges of lava fields and expose a beautiful columnar structure in the lava, as well as a number of watercourses. Also it is very common to see a row of springs, usually marked by brilliantly green moss-patches, coming to light in a mountain side. This usually signifies a layer of impenetrable clay that hinders the water in sinking further.

Waterfalls are very common in mountainous Iceland and they have every conceivable shape and form. Often the small waterfalls are the prettiest, with a high fall into a pool from which several outlets form a number of smaller waterfalls on the same level. Whereas Dettifoss impresses one with its terrifying power, Skogafoss is so perfectly proportioned that one does not realize that it is about 200 feet high. It also presents itself very well for one stands at its foot and can follow the water falling in white garlands gradually dissolving into spray with a rainbow. Many people think Gullfoss the most beautiful of our waterfalls and others vote for Fjallfoss. The waterpower available in Iceland is estimated at four million horse power, of which only a fraction has been put to use.

There is also a great number of lakes in Iceland. The largest are Thingvallavatn, which is about 27 square miles and over 300 feet deep, Thorisvatn, and Myvatn, which is only 11 feet deep. They are nearly as variable as the waterfalls, for we have some of the long basins scooped out by a glacier as Skorradalsvatn, circular crater lakes and large areas where a glacier has retired so recently that every depression is filled with water which has not found any proper outlet yet, as at Tvidaegra.

As a modern house has hot and cold water, Iceland is similarly furnished. In addition to the cold water it has also a hot water system. Also it has several springs with icy cold mineral water (containing carbonic acid) in Snaefellsnes. When these different hot and cold water systems intermingle, somewhat strange situations may arise. It is in the main true that one can fish boiled trout there. In a brook at Laugar one can see shoals of small trout disporting themselves. But the water is so hot that one cannot hold the hand in it. The explanation is that the boiling hot water from a nearby spring floats on top of a cold brook in which the trout swim. If a trout is pulled through the layer of hot water, it is slightly boiled but left there somewhat longer it can be boiled through.

The natural hot springs have for centuries been used for bathing and washing and lately the water of a hot spring 12 miles from Reykjavik

*Gullfoss: The golden waterfall*

has been piped into town where it has been connected with the central heating of the houses and used to heat them. This has saved import of coal and left all the chimneysweeps unemployed, making the town much cleaner than it was when every house had a fire in the furnace during the winter.

Probably there are thousands of these hot springs. How many there are we cannot say, for where there is subterraneous heat a small hole in the ground may soon fill with hot water. Some are high up in the mountains under the glacier ice and inaccessible. Some are out at sea, and for centuries the fishermen of the isles of Breidafjordur have gone to these to replenish their supply of fresh water.

The aristocrats of this family are the geysers that erupt at intervals and throw great masses of hot water high into the air. Like the glaciers this phenomenon was unknown in Europe until Iceland was discovered, and the fame of Geysir was such that the name of this Icelandic spring has been given to all other hot springs that erupt, and to a number of useful household appliances and bath water heaters besides.

The Great Geysir of Iceland is the largest of these springs. It is situated in an area with a number of hot springs each with its individuality and peculiarity. The water deposits white sinter. This sinter has built up a white hill with a circular basin in the top, filled with deep blue water nearly boiling. In the center of the basin which is about 60 feet across is a pipe 11 feet wide and over 70 feet deep into the earth. The water in the pipe is superheated to about 270° F. At some alteration in balance the water suddenly changes into steam with such violence that the water on top is thrown 120-180 feet in the air, but the column has been measured at as much as 220 feet high. This gigantic fountain is a waterfall in reverse. It is one of the most majestic sights in this world.

No justice can be done to the Icelandic landscape without mentioning the birds that enliven it with their bright colours, endearing music and pleasant family life. Here, however, only a few can be mentioned.

Of the fauna the birds are by far the most numerous and make up for the paucity of other fauna. The Icelanders are great lovers of birdlife and many birds are preserved by law, but many more by the unwillingness of the inhabitants to destroy any life and especially that of birds. They are absolutely unable to regard the killing of birds as sport. The ptarmigan has been caught in winter for food, however, and many of

*Geysir in eruption*

the sea birds too. Even when swans accumulate by the thousands and destroy meadows no Icelander would dream of firing a shot at them.

The Icelandic falcon was renowned all over Europe when falconry was the sport of kings, and for many years the standard of the king of Iceland was a blue field with a silver falcon. They are mentioned as gifts from the king to other royalties all over Europe and even to Arab kings. The Icelandic falcon has therefore always been protected, but the stealing of the young was a royal prerogative and all other poachers were severely punished.

The falcon is a brilliant pirate of the air and to see it fight is an unforgetable experience. Its extreme swiftness in overtaking, stunning the victim with one blow, and digging its talons into it before it falls is like seeing a feathered bolt of lightning. Its piercing war cry when it digs its beak into the breast of its prey gives the spectacle a sinister ferocity. Specialists tamed the falcons so that these fierce birds came at the call of their masters even when they were so far away that they were invisible. The Icelandic falcons, which can attain a stature of three feet, were such superior fighters that it is told of a French King that after having seen one fight, he did not enjoy seeing any other hawks fight, not even the peregrine. As it is the biggest of the hawks, it was preferably pitted against the biggest of prey. Their stout hearts fought against any odds and if overwhelmed they fell with honor.

There used to be a number of whitetailed sea eagles in Iceland. In this century they have diminished very much, though one can occasionally see them sitting at a stream ready to pounce on a salmon or trout floundering in the shallows. They seem to rise very laboriously as if far too heavy for flying, and are not known to catch other birds in the air. When they have risen, they soar magnificently.

The whooper swan or whistling swan, as the Americans call it, because whooping has acquired a hilarious meaning not applicable to the dignity of this stately bird, is very common in Iceland. They are similar to the mute swan but lack the heavy boss at the base of the beak, and never arch their necks. They nest in many inland lakes on great piles of twigs and waterplants and can be seen for miles while nesting. They are extremely fierce birds, especially when the cygnets are small.

To see the swans in flight is a most impressive sight. They break up into bands and fly in wedge-shaped flocks each led by a clarion voiced

*Falcon at the eyrie*

veteran. Arising from the lakes with outstretched necks, they leave their mirrored reflections on the water and sail overhead like a heavenly regatta. Each bird has a spread of six to seven feet, and they appear unhurried though very rapid flyers and swimmers. The song, as we call it, is a trumpet-like sound, from deepest bass, presumably from the old leaders, to a clarionet with every note between, some of them in falsetto.

Formerly Icelanders collected the feathers as they were shed, but with the advent of fountain pens the quills are not much sought by commerce, though New College in Oxford still supplies its students with an expertly cut quill. The writing with a soft quill has a special charm, and most of those who have read old letters and manuscripts know the little thrill when the broad strokes of the worn quill suddenly change into the fine lines of the re-cut pen, reminding them of these fine birds.

In the autumns the swans gather by the thousands at the fjords and beaches and only a few leave Iceland in the wintertime.

The eider-duck is a half domesticated bird. The down commands an extremely high price, being the best in the world. The duck plucks it from its breast to line the nest and when the duck has hatched her eggs, people collect the nests. The birds seem to use the same sites for their nests year after year, and the farmers try to attract them to hatch on their land by protecting the colonies against any disturbance and creating a happy home atmosphere for the birds. They apparently have the same taste as people who enjoy amusement parks, because mirrors, tinsel and bright flags seem to be the most effective and irresistible attractions. The strikingly attired male is a most devoted husband and the union probably lasts for life. During the egg-laying he stands by the duck in the nest making a moaning conversation of: ha-ho, ha-ho, to which his better half answers with a prosaic: quack. While the duck is hatching the eggs, the drake sneaks away to join other drakes and seems a most uninterested and deplorable father. In the autumn the drakes can be found in colonies of thousands pleasantly rocking on the waves under cliffs and far out at sea. In justice to the male, however, it must be said that in summer they moult so excessively that they are at times unable to fly. The duck is a husky bird of 11 pounds when she begins sitting but when she proudly takes the ducklings to the sea for their first swim and meal she weighs scarcely more than five to six pounds.

Among the great number of ducks can be mentioned the mallard,

*The breeding eiderducks blend perfectly with the ground*

the widgeon, the harlequin, the pintail and the teal, the squaw with its clarinet-like trumpeting, Barrows Golden Eye and many more. There is a great number of grebe and merganser, but geese breed far inland at little lakes. Lake Myvatn is a duck paradise. The water is full of life and the lake is named after the midgets that come by the billions in two seasons, early spring and late summer. Whereas they try to eat up innocent humans, the trout in the lake feed on the larvae and the ducks on them and the trout fry. The worst killer of fry is the horned grebe which builds its nest afloat from twigs and can oft be seen sitting on the nest and paddling it along. Their headdress looks very ridiculous to men but quite stylish to women.

Of the moorbirds there used to be such profusion of ptarmigans that they ruined the hay, and one could not walk in certain areas for fear of stepping on the yellow and brown striped chickens. Some disease seems to have taken a terrific toll of them in 1918-19 and since then they are nothing like so numerous as they used to be though they are still common.

Probably the favorite bird of the Icelanders is the golden plover. When it arrives we say spring has arrived, for it winters in the Mediterranean or farther south and comes to Iceland in the last days of March. It has a rather sweet, mellow, plaintive song: deerin deerin deerin dee with the last note rising. Their intricate and beautiful evolutions in flight are a delight on an autumn day when the flocks are preparing for the migration. Its relative, the whimbrel, with its long bill, is another bird that gives Icelandic moors their peculiar melancholy note. Often it runs at a short distance from the traveller for a long time, stopping occasionally to look at him and issuing its long drawn out whistle.

Another bird fond of human society is the big black raven with the guttural croak and a wingspread of over four feet. In the autumn they pair off and one pair settles at each farm. They are supposed to be prophetic birds, especially harbingers of bad news for they seem to have some sense that tells them when a person is dying and a death house is often beset by a number of these birds that circle in flight over it, uttering their harsh cries.

In the cliffs at the sea a great number of birds breed, but their unmelodious voices and undistinguished habits do not awaken the same sympathy as that of the other birds.

The biggest of these birds is now extinct. It was the great Auk which could be considered the arctic analogue of the antarctic penguins. The last of these birds were killed off in Iceland in 1844. Their habitat is now occupied by great colonies of gannets that obviously like company, for they can hardly move without stepping on each other. They have a six-foot wingspread and are perfectly streamlined. They often plunge for food from a considerable height, sending up great fountains of spray.

The gulls form great colonies, and one often sees the cliffs spotted with thousands of them. The arctic tern, however, often breeds far inland. This bird spends its winter in the antarctic and it is supposed to fly not less than 25,000 miles a year, looking for the midnight sun. Its arrival in Iceland usually by 10th of May signifies that summer has arrived. The arctic skua breeds on black sands and wasteland and imparts a special haunting quality to these god-forsaken areas.

On the sheerest cliffs facing the ocean live the guillemots and murres and lay their eggs on the smallest of sills where there is a constant draft. The eggs are, however, so made that they cannot blow off though they roll from one side to another. On the grassy tops of such cliffs the puffins dig long burrows with their fantastic bill. This nose in red and orange would give them a very drunken appearance, if it were not for some sober gray stripes. The bill, however, has many uses for one can often see puffins flying home with from eight to twelve small fishes that have been worked into the elastic rosette at the corner of the mouth.

Many of the Icelandic birds migrate to the American East Coast while others follow age old routes over Britain or to the east of Ireland, supposedly routes laid out when the land was still above water.

It is doubtful whether any species of mammals but the blue fox is indigenous, though one kind of mouse possibly is. Reindeer were introduced in 1771 and live in inaccessible places in the interior, but have never had any economic importance for the Icelanders.

A recent addition to the fauna is the mink. They were imported by ranchers, but some of them escaped and have enjoyed their freedom thoroughly. They seem to have increased in number to an incredible degree. In spite of its prosperous looking and expensive fur Icelanders have not taken to the newcomer. They disapprove of its character. In their henhouses it has engaged in wanton slaughter. They fear it will ruin the salmon fisheries and depopulate the bird colonies.

Seals and whales used to be common but with this century and the increased number of ships and steamers they have rapidly diminished. Seals, however, are common, especially at salmon rivers and they sometimes chase salmon far up into the inland. On sunny days they can be seen sunning themselves on flat rocks looking in the distance like small boats with their heads and tails out of the water. They are intelligent animals with beautiful brown eyes. They love music and bright colours and often follow boats for a long time to feast their eyes on a red garment and their ears on the music of an accordion.

The whales of value in human commerce are now very scarce at Iceland. There are, however, still a few of these huge mammals in Icelandic waters, and the smaller whales are common. In the summer one can sometimes see a fjord which apparently overnight has been filled with dark, elongated islands. These are whales feeding on herring, swallowing them by the hundreds.

*The delta of Eyjafjardará*

The inferior fauna is only inadequately known and will not be treated here.

The soil of Iceland is, like most volcanic soil, very fertile, but light and porous. When Iceland was discovered the Sagas say it was covered with woods, which have since been exterminated by a people in dire need of wood for fuel and building purposes.

This is most likely true. The form of the landscape shows that it used to be wooded, and numerous charcoal pits are found on hills covered with heather where now not a tree is visible. The black snail, a typical dweller of woods, is still found in considerable numbers on moors, e.g. on Mossfellsheidi. Now only sad remnants of the woods that formerly

*Godafoss — Waterfall of the Gods*

covered Iceland remain and they are mostly in inaccessible places where neither man nor sheep can get at them. For while man cut down the best trees, the sheep roamed the woods and destroyed the young plants.

The best remnants of the Icelandic woods have been made preservations during this century and are now valuable as a source of seeds of these indigenous trees. The largest of these preservations is Hallormstadaskogur on the East Coast, where the birches reach a height of about 30 feet, while spruce and fir, which is imported, are 15-20 feet. Baejarstadaskogur, which is so inaccessible, between glaciers and a swift river, that it has survived, has probably the best species of Icelandic birches. We love these wooded areas. Not only because of their rarity, but because they are very pleasant spots. In many woods the slender rowan trees are

*Towards evening*

common with their clusters of flowers and later of red berries, much sought after by the thrushes. Both trees give plenty of light so that the ground is covered with a thick carpet of grass, flowers, crowberries and blueberries, while wild strawberries are common in some of the woods.

The wild flowers in Iceland are small with short stem and bright blooms. The brightness of the colors is by some ascribed to the intense light that the plants enjoy during the spring when the sun is above the horizon over 20 hours of the day.

The most important part of the flora for the inhabitants are the grasses and sedges, which serve as fodder for the animals. The grasses are of very good quality as fodder, especially those that grow on the manured fields round the farms, largely composed of tufted hair-grass.

*A farm with oldfashioned turf stables*

In the spring the lambs and foals are earmarked and turned loose with their mothers in the highlands. As spring progresses the green tender growth appears higher and higher and the animals follow the young plants ever farther up the mountains, always grazing on the tenderest new grass. It seems the animals love this life, and when spring comes, there is no holding them in the lowlands and the lambs develop very rapidly on the short mountain grass. All the lowlands of Iceland are covered with grass, but the flora seems to change remarkably little from the lowlands to the highlands. The same flowers and grasses as are found round the farms of the lowlands grow also high in the mountains. Close to the glaciers and on mountain-tops over 3400 feet high are found the same cheerful buttercups and willows as by the coast. The best birch-

*Laxa in Thingeyjarsysla — a salmon river*

wood grows at a height of over 1200 feet above sea level. Whether this means that most of the flora of the present day has survived the last phase of the Glacial Age is anybody's guess, but it seems likely. In North America plants could migrate from the south after the Glacial Age was over, but that would be impossible in Iceland. Some seeds are easily carried by birds, but in Iceland it seems that several plants live only in a limited area and have not spread from there.

Poppies are common but have not been found in the western part of Southern Iceland, while certain other plants, e.g. a kind of pea, is found only there. One of the two kinds of indigenous roses has been found only at Kvisker, which probably has been a Nunatak in the Glacial Age. The grasses wither early in the autumn indicating adjustment to a harder

*Stock in a garden*

climate than now. All this seems to show that the present flora is of a quality below that which the climate would call for if plant migration had taken place to any appreciable extent, and this is also indicated by the excellent growth of many imported plants.

Of the higher plants we now know of between 400 and 500. They seem to be organized in plant societies, principally according to the consistency and humidity of the soil. In the very wet soil at the valley bottom or in shallow ponds grow the sedges, some of which can attain a height of two to three feet in a few weeks. Where drainage is better come the grasses. In many valleys, especially the narrower ones, the vegetation changes abruptly at a certain height where birch and willow, blueberries and crowberries and all the plants we find in the wooded areas get pre-

*A corner of a garden*

ponderance over the grasses. This same picture can be repeated at different levels. The dry moors are covered with this varied growth, which
often indicates that underneath there is a porous lava stream that furnishes drainage.

The short, hardy grasses of Iceland are under certain circumstances
apt to form knolls that are the bane of the farmers, for where they appear
the haymaking is much more difficult and it is impossible to use machin-
ery for mowing and drying the hay. We do not know the cause of these
knolls, but several theories have been advanced.

Owing to the porosity of the soil, all vegetation on hills is apt to
show signs of lack of water in spite of the considerable rain in Iceland.
This stunted growth is especially visible on the eastern part of hills where

*Showing the half grown bananas*

the dew has dried off in the early morning sun. During dry spells these spots can form a hole in the carpet of vegetation, which the wind soon enlarges. Since Iceland lost its covering of trees it has suffered greatly from wind erosion. In one week in the spring of 1881 a great storm swept away the carpet of vegetation of a well wooded area of several square miles and denuded it of all soil down to the bedrock, which was an old lava stream. For a long time the lava stream was without vegetation, but gradually life began to work on it. Extremely slow-growing lichens attach themselves to the stones. Of these we know at least 230 species. Soon moss begins to form in patches on the lichens, first as fine as velvet but gradually bigger kinds grow. Of mosses we know about 300 species and of fungi about 550, but the lower orders have not been thoroughly inves-

*A stone covered with lichens and moss*

tigated. The mosses often form a bed over three feet deep and act as a dust trap, forming soil for the higher plants.

The wind erosion on the highlands is very considerable. Whereas the highlands used to be covered with varied growths of willow, birch and heather, it seems the sheep have in many places ruined this vegetation so that they are now rapidly being eroded. On Kjolur between Langjokull and Hofsjokull one sees small willows with four to six inches of root laid bare, and this indicates how much of the soil has been blown away since the plant began to grow there.

This dust collects in the valleys where it forms soil often of great thickness. In some parts of Fljotshlid the soil is nine feet deep.

*Grandfather teaches botany in his garden*

# THE ICELANDERS

Iceland was settled by Norsemen and Westmen in the ninth century. The Norsemen were Scandinavians, mostly from Norway with a sprinkling from other Scandinavian countries.

The Westmen were the people of the British Isles and Ireland. Unfortunately, we know very little of their settlement, but it seems that the South-East Coast of Iceland was fairly well settled by Christian Irishmen when the Norse came to Iceland in the middle of the ninth century. Several Celtic names still survive, but apart from these, the settlement of the Westmen has had little influence on the culture and language.

*Having the teddy photographed*

The Norsemen often captured slaves in Ireland and Scotland and brought them to Iceland. These were people of free birth and sometimes even high birth. Generally it is accepted that 70 per cent of the settlers were Norsemen and 30 per cent Westmen, but the blood classification of modern Icelanders seems to indicate a higher proportion for the Westmen.

In the ninth century there was considerable civil strife in Norway. The tyrant, King Harald Fairhair, defeated the lesser kings one after the other and subjugated them. Many of the defeated chiefs, called Jarls, preferred to emigrate with their families rather than accept the lordship of King Harald. Some of them went to Scotland, Ireland, and the Hebrides.

*Bessastadir.  The residence of the President of Iceland.*

But most went directly to Iceland, where they were later joined by many of those that had gone west from Norway.

The distinguished professor of Geography at Yale, Dr. Huntington, describes the settlers of Iceland thus:

"The original Icelanders were a highly selected group of people. In the first place, the Norse as a whole appear to be one of the world's competent races. Second, the Jarls were Jarls because their ancestors had shown unusual ability to fight, to organize, and to hold their conquests, and they themselves maintained their position largely by virtue of an inheritance of ability. Third, from among this most gifted group in an uncommonly able race there was selected first those who loved freedom

*The entrance to Bessastadir*

more than the favor of kings, and second those who were inclined to try their chances in a new and difficult land rather than gain a living by fighting and plundering. Thus it was the best of the best who founded Iceland, and they created there what Bryce calls 'an almost unique community whose culture and creative power flourished independently of any favoring material conditions and indeed under conditions in the highest degree unfavorable.' ''

The settlers, however, described the country very attractively. It was covered with a good-sized woods of birch and mountain ash. It was full of birds. The fjords and rivers teemed with fish. The animals had no fear of man. The virgin land was very fertile.

*Skiers*

They established a Republic with local assemblies and in 930 a central parliament called Althing. This was a most remarkable institution, for during the darkest age of Europe, when kingship was the only known form of Government, Icelanders had trial by jury and a parliament 300 years before the English established the "Mother of Parliaments." The British delegation that came to Iceland for the Millennium celebration of the Althing in 1930 graciously gave the Althing the title: "Grandmother of Parliaments."

The Althing was the juridical assembly as well as the legislative one. Justice was in the hands of a jury of twelve men of good repute. Punishment was usually a fine or banishment. The individual, whether man or

*The home made sweater*

woman, had the greatest protection in all matters of safeguarding their honor. Even a slave had certain rights, and the same rights as the free-born if he had to defend the honor of his womenfolk. After the adoption of Christianity slavery fell into disrepute and was soon abolished.

The settlers left their old homes in very small open boats. These were the Viking ships. A good sized Viking ship was 50 feet long and 10 feet broad but most were much smaller. It carried one big clumsy main sail made of tweed. In comparison the Mayflower would look like a liner to us. On these tiny craft the settlers sailed across a wide and rather rough ocean without maps or compass. Owing to the smallness of the ship, each family could carry only absolute necessities. Food and water for

*The fisherman's daughter*

the crew and passengers would take up most of the space.

The settlers had to dispose of all their property when they left their homeland. They were interested in taking silver, gold, good weapons and similar goods of high value compared with their bulk.

When they arrived in Iceland, everybody had silver and it was, therefore, of little value there. In Scandinavia and Britain, depleted by the large export to Iceland, it had a high price. In Iceland it was so abundant that the owners of the temples covered the beams with silver and Egill Skallagrimsson returned a sword with silver incrustations which he received from a king as a present with the blunt explanation that he had enough of inferior swords.

Such a situation calls forth a lively commerce. Many foreigners sailed to Iceland with their precious cargo and exchanged it for silver. Icelanders went abroad and lived in fine style on the silver their fathers and grandfathers had brought to Iceland. This wealth made them feel rather grand. When some ships stranded, a steward who was a serf invited all the sailors to stay at his master's estate and refused to take any payment. When reproved by the master, the steward answered: "While Iceland is settled the greatness of that man will be remembered whose slave dared to do this without permission." The master answered: "For this action I give you your freedom and this estate which you have taken care of."

There was great hospitality. A landowner built a house across the main road to be sure that no travellers should pass his estate hungry or thirsty. There were also grand parties, especially at midwinter when a hundred guests or more were invited. It was a poor party that lasted less than 3 days and where each guest did not receive a gift from his host. Wedding parties lasted a week with a definite program for each day.

The daily clothes were of homemade tweed, but for parties splendid foreign clothes were worn, in good colors and of fashionable cut. Thick armrings of silver were worn both by men and women, and heavy brooches fastened their cloaks together. This jewelry was adorned with elaborate patterns showing allegorical and mythological figures, especially dragons and snakes biting their tails with a malice that did not even spare their own body. Such vermin had the nature to make metal grow and changed shape easily for these adornments were also used as money.

The houses also were handsomely decorated, and many colored tapestries were hung on the walls. The beams were carved and painted and at the seat of the master of the household were the carved columns brought from the old family home in Norway.

Conversation and story telling were the chief amusement, together with the recitation of poetry. To the modern mind it seems odd that the composition of insulting verses and of love songs should be classed together as a punishable offence. But each was an infraction of the privacy of the individual. The hand of a young daughter should be sought in a seemly way from the parents, who would consult the daughter. It is often mentioned that a strong love united the couple after marriage, but before marriage any show of feelings was frowned upon.

Several of the settlers were Christians but by far the most were heathens. They believed in Odin (Wotan), and Thor and their family. This was rather a rough clan. The lays of the Eddas, the only surviving mythology, were written down by Christians, and it is possible that they have not been fair to the fallen deities. That is apt to happen. We do not really get the impression, either from Sagas or Eddas that the people believed in the gods. They tried to strike a bargain with them, and we are told that some of them made promises to Thor for protection on sea journeys and perilous enterprises. Nor would he be much use else-where because he is described as a god of unlimited strength and equally unlimited stupidity.

The individual is carried along by fate, but fate is twofold; forlög which come from above, his gifts of mind and heart and body; örlög, the fate of surroundings and environment. He must make the best of both. If a man clashes with somebody else, that is fate. But he may also clash with himself. Even the best can have the bad luck not to fit into his sur-roundings. The Saga of Grettir tells of such a man. Whatever fate has to offer you, you must accept with manliness:

> Cattle die, and kinsmen die,
> And so one dies one self;
> One thing I know that never dies
> The fame of a dead man's deeds.

It seems that the old belief did not satisfy the religious needs of the Icelanders. We are told of some heathens who worshipped Him who had created the sun. They were so ready for the teachings of Christianity, that it spread like wildfire. Some Icelanders had heard of Christianity abroad. The first Christian missionaries arrived in Iceland and told of their faith in 981 A.D. Nineteen years later, in the year 1000 A.D., Christianity was adopted as the State religion. Public worship of the heathen gods was made a punishable offense, but private worship was allowed to those who could not adopt the new religion.

In the same year that Iceland adopted Christianity, a young Ice-lander, Leif Erikson was converted in Norway where he was on a short journey. He was probably born at Eiriksstadir in Haukadal, where Icelanders still point out the grassgrown ruin of a house, supposed to be built by his father, Erik the Red. When Leif was an infant Erik left home to explore the countries to the west of Iceland. He was away for three years and sailed far north along the West Coast of Greenland, and probably also along the North Coast of America into the Hudson Bay. He founded a settlement on the East Coast of Greenland, where there are ruins of several churches and many houses.

Leif Eriksson was anxious to convert his family to Christianity and took some priests with him to Greenland. On the way he missed the southern point of Greenland and sailed on until he came to the American mainland where he spent some time and built a house, in Wineland, which was probably the area from Boston to Newport, R. I. Cape Cod is called Kjalarnes (Keel peninsula) because it is formed like the keel of a ship, and the area of Narragansett Bay is called Straumfjordur (Stream firth) because of the many streams in the bay.

The Sagas mention five journeys to Wineland. One of these was led by a chief, Thorfinnur Karlsefni, who intended to settle there with his young wife. Their son: Snorri, was the first white child born in what is now United States territory, in 1004 A.D. His parents, however, moved back to Iceland, and founded a big family there, and many Icelanders now living, can trace their ancestry to Snorri. Though only five journeys are mentioned in the Sagas, there is little doubt that many more took place, and in 1347 the Icelandic annals mention a ship coming from Markland, which was the area north of Wineland. Apart from the many Icelandic sources, which describe the new lands in detail, the discovery is mentioned in the works of the eleventh century historian, Adam of Bremen.

*Statue in Philadelphia by the sculptor Einar Jonsson*

Several annals mention that in 1121 an Icelander who was bishop of Greenland, Erikur Upsi, went in search of Wineland, and he is thought to have built the "old tower of Newport" which is still standing and is probably the ruin of a round church of the type built in Scandinavia in the beginning of the twelfth century.

In 1930 United States donated to Iceland a statue of Leif Eriksson by Sterling Calder with the inscription: Leif Eriksson, Son of Iceland, Discoverer of Wineland, thereby officially acknowledging him as the discoverer of the vast continent of America.

The golden age lasted from 930 to 1030. It is called the Saga period.

After that it became fashionable to write down the doings of the ancestors. The Sagas are family histories, about forty in number, but besides there are many short stories. They are rather unequal in value, but some of them rank high in world literature, though they probably have been written by people not conscious of creating great art, and all are anonymous. The best of them show an art of story-telling which has probably not been equalled anywhere, until in the 19th century.

When each person is introduced his ancestors are enumerated and something told of them, because the Icelanders have always been greatly interested in their forefathers and in genealogy. In a weak State the family upheld the honor of its members. Then the writer tells what he knows about the members of the family in a clear direct style, without interposing his views or opinions. They do not seem interested in flattering the persons described, because as Snorri Sturluson said: Exaggerated praise is derogatory to the recipient. But sometimes they go a bit out of their way to tell of a happy rejoinder or a little trick. The best of the Sagas is the Saga of Burnt Nial, well translated by Dasent.

All we know of the mythology of the Norsemen is from the Eddas. The Elder or Poetic Edda is a collection of mythological and heroic songs, while the Younger or Prose Edda contains treatises on mythology, language, and the art of versemaking by Snorri Sturluson (1178-1241).

All these books were written in Icelandic at a time when all learning in Europe expressed itself in the Latin language. The Latin precluded the common man from partaking in the culture of the higher classes. But in Iceland the wisdom and culture of the ancestors was available in the native tongue. For centuries the Sagas were read in the country, while the

*A pageant representing the first parliament in 930 A. D.*

masters and servants alike sat at their handicrafts, whether it was carving, preparing the wool, or repairing tools. This not only enriched the language of the people but widened their horizon. When the reader paused, the audience discussed the people described, and lauded or censored their acts, thus forming the character and opinion of the younger people, giving them a feeling of their common heritage. We have scores of volumes of the sagas that have been handwritten at great expense and with long hours of labor. These old parchment tomes of hundreds of pages have long ago lost their pristine whiteness. They are now brown with age and smoke and the handling of hundreds who have read them and loved them and assimilated them as a cultural treasure.

As time went on the silver left the country. Commerce was one-sided for three centuries, and traders were reluctant to go to distant Iceland to obtain only farm produce and dried fish such as could be obtained elsewhere. Trade was not in the hands of Icelanders. Temperamentally they were not suited for commerce. Neither did they have the timber to build or repair ships. By 1200 A.D. the most clear sighted saw isolation looming as a threatening ogre. Besides the commercial isolation, spiritual isolation also reared its head. The church regarded monarchy as the natural form of Government. Iceland, which was in the archdiocese of Norway, was under a strong pressure both from the throne and from the Church to accept the king of Norway as king of Iceland. The Archbishop even refused to consecrate bishops to the diocese in Iceland, unless they worked for the establishment of monarchy there.

In 1262 A.D. Icelanders agreed to pay the king of Norway a tax on their land against his promise to give them full rights in Norway and send six ships to Iceland every summer with foreign goods. This was, therefore, an insurance agreement against isolation, and there was no acceptance of any divine overlordship, for it is expressly stated: "This agreement we and our descendants will keep in good faith so long as you also faithfully keep it, but we consider ourselves released from all obligations, if, in the opinion of the best men, it shall be broken."

Though the Icelanders reserved to themselves the right to decide whether it was broken it soon became of little worth to them. But for centuries this treaty was the basis of the Icelandic struggle for freedom against the encroachment of power by the king, who more and more

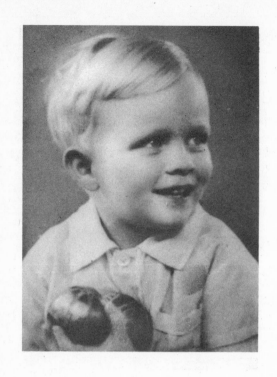 

*The hope of the future*

came to represent foreign rather than Icelandic interests.

In 1381 all the four Scandinavian States were united under one king. This turned out to be a disaster for all these freedom loving people. In 1520 Sweden took its own king, in 1814 Norway separated from Denmark. In 1918 Denmark recognized Iceland as a free and independent State and made a treaty to decide whether any ties would be of advantage to both countries after a trial period of 25 years.

During this union of the Scandinavian States none of them lost its existence as a State. When the king usurped the power of the parliaments and ruled as an absolute monarch, there was little political freedom. It survived longest in Iceland, however, for during all the darkest ages of royal power the Althing met yearly and pronounced judgment according to the ancient laws, setting aside any royal decree that a jury deemed unsuitable or injurious to Icelandic interests. It was not till 1800 that the king dissolved the Althing and set up a court with Danish-trained lawyers to exercise the judicial functions. The Althing was, however, re-established in 1843 and is now the legislative assembly of a fully sovereign Republic.

Though Iceland fared better politically than the other Scandinavian States in the middle ages, and the flame of learning and culture shone brighter there than in most other European countries, it fared badly economically. The great epidemics that swept Europe also reached Iceland, but the greatest disaster was man-made. In 1602 the king gave his Danish subjects a monopoly on trading with his Icelandic subjects.

The prices were so high that the Danish traders bragged of the fact that they made good profits even though one of every four ships were lost. The loss to Iceland was, however, many times greater than the profits of the traders for during generations it was difficult to get the elementary things for carrying on agriculture and fisheries, such as lumber for repairing the fishing boats and iron for scythes. The best-paying cargo was brandy and that was usually available to the great detriment of the population.

The ensuing poverty was degrading. The people were on the verge of starvation. Their resistance to disease was nil. After an eruption in 1783-4 which ruined the grass in large areas, they lost their livestock and one fifth of the population died of hunger in the years 1784-85. Then at last the bonds of the trade monopoly were slackened, but they were not removed entirely until 1854.

During the Napoleonic wars the British broke into this trade

*The coming generation is studious and wears the national dress*

monopoly and forced the king's officers to make a treaty allowing free trade. In return the king of Great Britain issued an Order in Council on February 7th, 1810, directing that Icelanders should be considered as "stranger friends" and "in no case as alien enemies." This is probably the first time that the subjects of a king at war with another nation have been given this status, and one hopes to find a wider application of it in the future for unfortunate people who are hurled into wars by the ambitions of a tyrant.

This Order in Council applied to the peoples of Greenland and the Faroe Islands as well as to Iceland. It seems that at the peace making of 1814 the British thought these countries outside the power of the King of Denmark. The peace terms, therefore, specified only that Norway was taken from his domain. Iceland and his other possessions soon came back under his rule, for the Icelanders were obviously unprepared to take over the Government of their country.

Icelanders had to work out their own salvation. It came through their ancient culture. Jonas Hallgrimsson, the great poet, revived the language. His friend, Tomas Saemundsson, preached the economic regeneration, but both of them died young, Jonas 38 years old in 1845, Tomas 34 years old in 1841. Their life work was carried on by Jon Sigurdsson (1811-79), the beloved leader of Iceland. His birthday, June 17th, is a national holiday. It has been chosen as day of good augury, for the re-establishment of the Republic.

He is probably unique among the many national leaders of the nineteenth century. The son of a country parson, he was the least martial of men. He never carried arms. He was a quiet scholarly man, who loved books and manuscripts. He published excellent editions of the classical literature, but also a great number of newer books through the Literary Society of Iceland, of which he was the leading genius all his life and which still publishes the oldest periodical in Scandinavia.

His historical research convinced him not only of the legal rights of the Icelanders but of their need for freedom. He began to publish a periodical for social science. The mainstay of each volume was a long precise and learned dissertation on the economy and the rights of Icelanders and their necessity for free trade and self-government. Today we would perhaps not regard it as very effective propaganda. It never stretches a point. It does not use catch phrases. But it worked strongly on his compatriots. Soon they began to ask for more freedom from the king. They were modest and polite, but every year now this meet-

*Jon Sigurdsson. "The pride of Iceland, its sword and shield"*

ing or that district sent in a petition for freedom. They were supported by the Danish liberals. In 1843 the Althing was re-established as an advisory body. In 1848 Denmark got its Constitution and there it was decided that Icelanders should have representatives in the Danish assembly. This was a great disappointment. Iceland was a separate State, and it was purely accidental that their king was also king of Denmark. He was like a man administrating two estates. The heirs to each had the right to demand that their heritage should be administrated separately. One could not be merged into the other. They could not be administrated as a single unit with justice.

At last, in 1874, Iceland received its own Constitution, with a restricted home rule. The estate, of which the people could now share the management, was not worth much. The country had been sucked dry in the evil days of economic exploitation. There was not a single mile of road in Iceland. Not a bridge. Apart from a few poor churches there was only one public building. That was the prison.

In 1904 Iceland secured home rule. From that year real progress began, and the standard of life improved rapidly. In 1874, for example, the exports from Iceland amounted to 3.2 million kronas; by 1904 they had risen to 10.4 million kronas and in 1944 to 254 million kronas.

The constitutional struggle ended with the Union Treaty of 1918. Iceland was then recognized as an independent and sovereign State. There was, however, a strong feeling in Iceland that the head of the State should be an Icelander, elected by the nation. During wars Iceland was always cut off from its king. When we most needed the chief executive, he was inaccessible, and we had to avail ourselves of makeshift arrangements. This happened in World War I, and as soon as the Germans invaded Denmark in 1940, Icelanders again lost all connection with their king. Under the very trying conditions of the German occupation of Denmark, King Christian X became a national hero and revealed himself a man of great stature. Peculiarly enough this strengthened the desire of the Icelanders for their own head of State. For it showed us what we were missing in our national life in not having our own chief executive, familiar with all aspects of Icelandic life. After the occupation of Denmark, the Althing entrusted the royal functions to the Cabinet. Later a chief executive was elected, but out of respect to the king, he was called regent.

*Sveinn Bjornsson. The President of Iceland*

In May 1944 a general referendum was held at which 95 per cent of the population over 21 years of age declared themselves in favor of a Republican Constitution. On June 17th the Republic of Iceland was proclaimed in the presence of special ambassadors representing the President of the United States, the King of England, the King of Norway and other dignitaries. The King of Denmark sent his former subjects a message of good wishes, which was received with enormous enthusiasm.

Immediately after the proclamation the Honorable Sveinn Bjornsson was inaugurated President. He is a man of ancient Icelandic lineage, who has rendered his country great services, both as leader in its economic life and in his post as Minister and Envoy Plenipotentiary of Iceland.

The young Republic was recognized immediately by the Allied Nations. President Roosevelt also invited President Bjornsson on an official visit to the United States in August 1944, an act greatly appreciated by all Icelanders.

Though being only about 125,000 in number, the Icelanders face the future without fear for their State. We feel that because of our love of freedom we will always follow the same course as the great Democracies that were godparents at the re-establishment of our Republic. Nazi Germany received its first blunt refusal of co-operation from Iceland in the spring of 1939. A big commission was sent there to negotiate air bases. These were of course to be strictly "civilian and commercial." The Icelandic cabinet, presided over by Hermann Jonasson, refused to allow the Germans to extend their air lines to Iceland and to build air bases there. This was at a time when other nations were making non-aggression pacts with the Nazis. Then Germany officially asked to be given opportunity to make tenders for great public works that were being prepared in Iceland. They promised beforehand a cheaper offer than anybody else and unlimited credit facilities. They never received the opportunity. We did not wish to have a number of German technicians in Iceland under any pretext. In this strong resistance to German infiltration Iceland played a role which everybody sees now was of importance to world history. Nobody can say what would have been the outcome of the Battle of the Atlantic if the Nazis had had a footing in the "unsinkable aircraft carrier," as Iceland was called by them.

On May 10th, 1940, the British landed a force of Marines in Iceland and fortified the country, thereby placing it outside the grasp of the

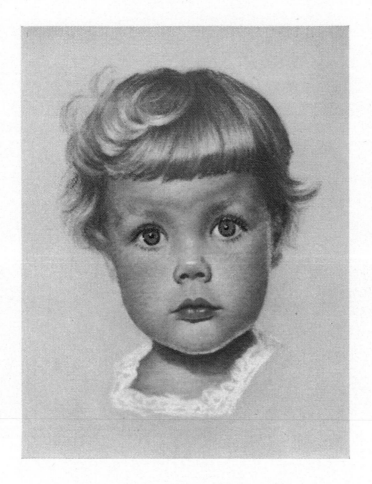

*Two year old (A pastel by Zoe Shippen)*

Germans. At the same time they issued a Proclamation to the effect that this was done to forestall a German invasion. They pledged to respect the independence of Iceland and appointed an envoy with the rank of minister there. This pledge was scrupulously observed. The British never mixed in the internal affairs of Iceland and therefore never occupied it though they had bases there.

On July 7th, 1941, a Treaty between Iceland and the United States was made public. By this Treaty the United States agreed to give Iceland military protection during the war and withdraw its troops after the war was over. It recognized Iceland as a sovereign State and together with

*A tiny harbor*

Britain pledged that any Peace conference would recognize the full sovereignty of Iceland. On that same day a strong force of American troops landed there to relieve the British who were hard pressed elsewhere.

We do not know how many troops were stationed in Iceland. Guesses range usually between 60 and 90 thousand men. If these figures are right it means that the population increased by 50-75 per cent in a few months. All our facilities were therefore very inadequate. How inadequate the reader can see for himself if he imagines a similar increase in his own town or country. We had only a few small cinemas and few and small hotels. The troops suffered greatly from boredom. We were unhappy about this but could do nothing to relieve it. They had a great deal of money and very little to spend it on. Prices therefore rose very rapidly,

*Dettifoss: The most powerful waterfall in Iceland.*

and we had no power to stop this inflation. The army command wished to use Icelandic labor for such work as construction. Wages rose greatly, and agriculture lost much of its labor supply, dislocating trade. This was inevitable, but both the troops and Icelanders were inconvenienced by it.

Icelanders have not words enough to praise the behavior of the troops. It was very good indeed and we formed a very high opinion of the peoples of Britain and the United States which these boys represented. A few unpleasant incidents occurred, but whether they were one for every thousand troops or one for every ten thousand, we could not judge. Probably they were somewhere in between, which is a very fine record. The army command were always most cooperative and ready to solve any problems put up to them.

*The Study of President Sveinn Bjornsson*

The chief amusement of the troops was to invent tall stories for the benefit of new arrivals. A few of these got into print as facts, vouched for by individuals without a sense of humor. Soon the army command secured some extremely able liaison officers who instructed the troops and explained our ways to them and after that both the stories and other misunderstandings disappeared completely.

As mentioned above, the Icelanders are a mixture of Scandinavians and Celts. As practically no immigration has taken place for centuries, they are a very homogeneous people. This does not mean, however, that a special type of Icelanders has evolved, for humanity is as varied there as elsewhere. Most of them have fair or sandy hair and light complexions often with a sprinkling of freckles. Their eyes, which are rather

*The high school at Laugarvatn*

deep-set, are mostly grey, blue or bluish-grey. The face is long and narrow. They are as a rule slender and according to measurements probably the tallest of the European nations.

There are no class differences, and each man feels as good as his neighbour. Their sense of justice and independence is very strong. The most common praise in obituaries is to say that the deceased was a "drengur," a word as untranslatable as gentleman in English. The sense of the word which means boy, can best be given as a good scout, for the "drengur" in Icelandic is one that holds high the ideals of the scout movement of being fair to all, helpful to the weak, a good citizen, cooperative and upstanding, truthful and honest.

This striving for fairness, especially to those absent, who commonly

*Mrs. Blondal, the principal of a Domestic Science College*

are at fault, may often lead the Icelander into a heated argument for things which he really dislikes. His sympathy for the underdog may therefore give strangers an absolutely wrong impression of his real opinions, especially as he loves fencing with words and refuses to yield.

Icelanders are very kind to animals and love children. Any kind of cruelty or inflicting of pain, is abhorrent to them. Psychic faculties are common, both clair-voyance and clair-audience.

They are fond of reading and of poetry. Especially the older people have a fund of verses and epigrams from which they quote liberally in conversation and draw comfort in every exigency. A favorite game of the children was to cap verses, which consisted in reciting a ditty and challenging the adversary to quote another one beginning with the

*The College at Akureyri*

letter with which the preceding one ended.

The Icelanders are rather reserved with strangers, but at his trans-formation into a guest, their hospitality knows no bounds. This was both a virtue and a necessity in a country with scattered habitation and often great distances between the farms.

With improved standards of living in this century, health has improved very much. In 90 years the mean duration of life has increased by almost 25 years. In 1850-60 it was 32 years for men and 33 years for women. At present it is 56 years and 61 years respectively. In the years 1931-34 there were only 10.8 deaths per thousand of population. This is somewhat less than in the United States and less than in any European country, except Norway and Holland.

*A brook in snow*

The low death rate is primarily due to the low infant mortality, which has been less than in most countries in the world. We are rather proud that Iceland has for a considerable time been among the three or four countries leading in low mortality for infants in the first year of life, for this usually indicates a good standard of cleanliness and intelligence.

Among the causes of death the most common was tuberculosis, followed by senility, cancer and pneumonia. These accounted for about one-half of all deaths. Now tuberculosis is steadily declining, and the medical service has taken x-ray photos of entire communities to be able to combat the disease at the earliest stage. We lose many men in the prime of life at sea where so many find their occupation. In the war years

*Haymaking*

we lost distressingly many ships and men to German submarines, which could attack our unarmed ships without risk. Our losses were proportionately higher than those of most of the warring nations.

In each district of Iceland there is a physician paid by the State, but in the towns there are in addition practising doctors and specialists. A number of hospitals have been built during recent years, but the supply is not quite adequate yet.

Compulsory sickness insurance takes care of doctors' bills, hospital expenses, and most of the cost of the medicines. This is just one part of a fairly comprehensive system of social insurance that includes also accident and old age insurance.

One of Iceland's chief drawbacks is the scarcity of good building

*A hydro electric plant*

materials. The stone available is both soft and porous, and not good for building purposes unless mixed with cement, which has only been available in this century. Turf was therefore used as filling between the stones, and because lumber was often unobtainable and very expensive, a special building style was evolved. The farm houses were erected in individual units of one room each placed side by side. The gables were wooden and often five to eight in number, forming a saw-toothed façade. As human habitation they were most unsatisfactory. They were difficult to keep clean and lasted only for a generation, which meant that each generation had to build its houses anew. The wood had to be used again and again, because of its scarcity. But each time a house was rebuilt a few boards were unusable and the end of a beam had to be sawn off. Each new

*A hothouse using natural hot water*

house was smaller than its predecessor. By 1874, when Iceland secured some home rule, practically the whole population lived in hovels. In all the country there were perhaps a dozen houses over 100 years old, built of wood or stone.

We have therefore no tradition in building houses. Until 1914 people built of wood. Since the last war they have begun to build houses of concrete. We are not very proud of our houses nor of our streets. And that perhaps can go for most of the human construction of our country, whether it be buildings or roads or fences made by man.

Many of the poets sang the praises of the old farms with the many wooden gables. They looked friendly in the landscape, because they were made of the same materials as the surrounding hills. And they were

*Fording a river*

friendly, too, because the people who lived in them were kindhearted and hospitable and ready to make travelers as comfortable as they could. Now these old turf houses are rapidly disappearing. The new houses are unprepossessing in appearance. They are, however, frankly speaking, houses only on the outside. Inside they are the homes of nice people who love them and make them very cozy. Every home has good sized bookshelves, where one finds the most astonishing variety of books, often bought at considerable expense. Formerly many houses had a harmonium, which is now being replaced by a piano, and every home has a radio. Broadcasting is a State institution where all the leading men of Iceland speak and give lectures, which supplies music from Boogie-Woogie to Beethoven, and where languages also are taught. Soap-operas are

*View of Thingvellir with the water filled fissures*

unknown and so are the silver-tongued commentators of infinite wisdom. The radio is staid and somewhat paternal. It is the favorite butt of the brotherhood of letter-writers to newspapers.

On the whole the homes are modern with over-stuffed chairs, polished tables and flowers, both cut and grown in pots on the window sill. On the walls one very often finds paintings, mostly by Icelandic painters, for foreign prints are not enjoying the popularity of former years. Central heating is prevalent everywhere, and all new houses and apartments have a bathroom or a shower. Electricity is in use in all the towns, and there are plans for electrifying the whole country-side. Many individual farms have their own electric plant, often built locally and utilizing a nearby waterfall. Electric kitchens with an American refrig-

*A trout stream in Borgarfjordur*

erator and washing machine are now common.

Icelandic is one of the oldest literary languages still spoken and written in Europe. It stands in a similar position to the Nordic languages and English as does Latin to the Romanic languages. A thousand years ago it was spoken all over Scandinavia, Northern Germany and Eastern England. Many of the most indispensable words in English are the same as in Icelandic. These are the words of everyday usage, family, relationship, life and death, joy and sorrow. Icelandic has changed so little that school children read the Sagas for fun, though they are published with an archaic orthography.

All Icelandic words are pronounced with the stress on the first syllable. This means that any foreign word fits badly into the language, and

*Vaglaskogur. The clear air gives a limitless view.*

Icelanders stake their honor on translating every word they need from abroad into Icelandic. Even such technical words as have come into usage with radio and television are now Icelandic. Foreign languages are taught in schools in towns to children from the age of ten years and English is widely read and spoken.

Another survival from olden times is that we use the Christian name and the father's name to which is added son or daughter but as a rule do not use family names. A daughter of Leif Eriksson would be Hildur Leifsdottir, and that would not be changed when she married.

Education is compulsory for children between the ages of seven and fourteen and all instruction is free. There are elementary schools in every district but the higher schools and technical schools are mostly

*Midnight sun*

in the towns. The agricultural colleges, however, are in the country and there is a movement to establish high schools for the farming youth locally, especially where there are hot springs which can furnish the heat for the school buildings and for the swimming pool which is regarded as a necessity in every school, since swimming is a compulsory part of the curriculum. These country high-schools are often used as hotels during the long summer vacation.

In Reykjavik there is a university with faculties in theology, law and economics, medicine, engineering, philosophy and philology with special stress on Icelandic language and literature. The students number about 300. But apart from these, over 300 students are at present at American universities studying either subjects they cannot obtain in

*A swimming bath with natural hot water*

Iceland or postgraduate work. The Icelandic State is liberal in furnishing scholarships to those who study some subject which is regarded as necessary for the development of Icelandic trade and interests.

The State and municipalities support not only all the schools but a number of educational instituticns besides. The State has a publishing society that supplies books at cost price, because Icelanders are great book buyers and in 1942 spent on the average $23.00 per family on books published in Icelandic, apart from all foreign books. Also the State supports two radio stations and the Church.

The Icelandic Church is of the Lutheran denomination as the other Scandinavian Churches, and there are only about 1.5 per cent of other denominations. The Church has always been a great cultural influence and one of the duties of the parson was to visit every home in his parish once a year to see that children received proper schooling. Confirmation at the age of 14 was only granted those who could read and write. This meant that for generations there has been no illiteracy in Iceland, which was a seven day wonder to travelers who wrote about Iceland in the last century. But apart from that the clergy often had schools in the vicarages for those who wished for higher education and sent students who spoke Latin and Greek fluently, to the University of Copenhagen.

Above has been mentioned the classical literature of Iceland: The Eddas and the Sagas. In them are preserved all we know of the culture of the ancient Scandinavians and Germans. The interest in culture and learning was always great in Iceland, even during the most desperate poverty. Lord Bryce, the distinguished ambassador to Washington and interpreter of the American Constitution, visited Iceland in 1874. He writes that the Icelandic people has been "from the beginning of its national life, more than a thousand years ago, an intellectually cultivated people which has produced a literature both in prose and in poetry that stands among the primitive literatures next after that of ancient Greece if one regards both its quantity and its quality. Nowhere else, except in Greece, was so much produced that attained, in times of primitive simplicity, so high a level of excellence both in imaginative power and in brilliance of expression."

Since this was written Iceland has had a renaissance in literature and the arts. Several anthologies have been published in English, the latest of which is: "Icelandic Poems and Stories," edited by Professor Richard

*Reykholts school. A country high school*

Beck, and published in 1943, to which a reader must be referred, as an adequate treatment of the flourishing literature of Iceland would in any case fall outside the scope of this little book. Among Icelandic authors who have had some of their books translated into English can be mentioned: Jon Thoroddsen, Johann Sigurjonsson, Gunnar Gunnarsson, Gudmundur Kamban, Kristmann Gudmundsson and Halldor Kiljan Laxness.

Iceland has had a good crop of painters in this century, among whom the accepted leaders are: Asgrimur Jonsson, Jon Stefansson, and Johannes S. Kjarval. The best known among the younger painters are Finnur Jonsson, Jon Thorleifsson, Gunnlaugur Blondal, Kristin Jonsdottir, Eggert Laxdal, Eggert Gudmundsson, Johann Briem, Magnus Arnason, and his wife Barbara Morrow Arnason.

In sculpture Einar Jonsson is generally hailed as a master. His works are found in several European countries as well as in the United States and Canada, but almost all of them are collected in the museum which the Icelandic State erected to house his works in Reykjavik. Among other sculptors of merit are: Gudmundur Einarsson, Rikardur Jonsson, Asmundur Sveinsson and Miss Nina Saemundsson, who lives in California.

In music Professor Bjarni Thorsteinsson distinguished himself by collecting and publishing a wealth of old Icelandic folk melodies and writing a book on them, which is a classic. He was also a composer, principally of church music. Professor Sveinbjornsson has composed, among other works, the national anthem of Iceland. Other composers of note are: Sigfus Einarsson, Arni Thorsteinsson, Pall Isolfsson, Bjorgvin Gudmundsson, Sigvaldi Kaldalons, Sigurdur Thordarson, Jon Leifs and Hallgrimur Helgason.

The twentieth century has seen not only a revival of literature and the arts but also of learning and of science in Iceland. This falls mainly in two fields: Research into the history, literature and language of the Icelanders and research into the nature of Iceland.

The two first professors in Icelandic literature and language at the University of Iceland, established in 1911, were Bjorn M. Olsen, who wrote articles on a great number of historical questions, works, which still stand as classics, and Sigurdur Nordal, the inspired literary historian of Iceland, to whom all the younger scholars in that field are indebted.

*Behind the National Library is the National Theatre*

Among his pupils are his successor: Professor Einar O. Sveinsson, Professor Richard Beck of the University of North Dakota, Professor Stefan Einarsson of the John Hopkins University, and Professor Jon Helgason at the University of Copenhagen, who succeeded Finnur Jonsson, an extremely prolific author, among whose works can be mentioned a voluminous history of the classical literature and the scalds.

Professor Halldor Hermannsson of Cornell University stands apart in so far as his works are mostly written in English even though they deal exclusively with Icelandic history and bibliography, on which he is the outstanding authority. His monographs which are over 30 in number cover a wide field, but besides he has published a catalogue of books in

*Samsstadir. A modern farm*

Icelandic and on Icelandic subjects in three big volumes. Professor of the University of Iceland, Jon Jonsson Adils, has written several biographies, and a work on the Trade Monopoly. His successor, Dr. Pall Eggert Olason, is a specialist on the period of the reformation and the 17th century, but has also written a biography of Jon Sigurdsson in five volumes. Dr. Thorkell Johannesson and Vilhjalmur Th. Gislason have made extensive research into the economic history of Iceland. Bishop Jon Helgason wrote a large History of the Icelandic Church, as well as a number of biographies, mostly of the eminent personalities of the Church of Iceland. Dr. Hannes Thorsteinsson was a leading authority on personal history and genealogy. Chief Justice, Dr. Einar Arnorsson, and Dr.

*Cows coming home from the pasture*

Bjorn Thordarson have written on Icelandic law and constitution, as well as on a number of historical questions.

In the field of Natural Science we also have several prominent men. Professor Thorvaldur Thoroddsen has written several volumes on the geography and geology of Iceland. Dr. Helgi Pjeturss has published valuable papers on geology, but has lately confined his writings to philosophy and metaphysics. Among the younger geologists Palmi Hannesson, Dr. Trausti Einarsson, Johannes Askellson, Dr. Sigurdur Thorarinsson and Gudmundur Kjartansson have published works of great promise, while Dr. Thorkell Thorkellsson has written on the hot springs of Iceland, approaching the subject from the physical angle.

*Sheep in a sorting pen*

Stefan Stefansson and Dr. Helgi Jonsson, were the leading botanists of Iceland and their work seems to be ably taken up by Steindor Steindorsson and Dr. Askell Love. Magnus Bjornsson and Dr. Finnur Gudmundsson have written on the bird life. Dr. Bjarni Saemundsson has several volumes to his credit on zoology and ichthyology, and Arni Fridriksson is in spite of his youth, an internationally known authority on fish life.

According to the census of 1940, 31 per cent of the population of Iceland lives on agriculture, 15 per cent works in the fishing industry, and 21 per cent in other industries; 9 per cent work in communications and 7 per cent in commerce.

*The Icelandic horse. A noble servant of man*

The biggest industry of Iceland is therefore agriculture. The farms are usually not gathered in villages, but each farm stands apart in the middle of a field of cultivated grass, which furnishes the principal crop: hay. Besides this there is usually a potato patch and a vegetable garden, with some flowers and shrubs. Grain is not an important crop though barley, rye and wheat are grown on some farms with fairly good results.

Every Icelandic farm has cows, sheep and horses. In the lowlands the principal stock is cows, for here the country is very well suited for dairy farming. In the highlands the main stress is laid on sheep-raising, utilizing the vast moors for grazing. The horse has for centuries been the chief means of transportation. They are delightful animals, as surefooted as goats, intelligent and companionable.

The stock in Iceland is descended from animals brought in by the first settlers, without admixture of foreign blood. Sheep, however, have been imported occasionally in the last hundred years to improve the wool. The animals are all rather small, as they tend to be on islands, and it is disputed whether our horse should be classified as a horse or as a pony, for it is rarely over 14-15 hands.

The Icelandic dog is a fairly large spitz. In the country it is indispensable, but as it may be a link in carrying a certain disease, the keeping of dogs is prohibited in towns. Farms in some districts have goats and pigs as well as the usual barnyard fowl. As a sideline a number of farmers breed fur animals, the indigenous blue-fox, the silver-fox, and minks.

Where there are hot springs, hothouses have been erected, but peculiarly enough they grow mainly flowers to be sold as cut flowers in the towns. Some grapes, tomatoes, cucumbers and melons are also grown. There are several generations of Icelandic bananas, which have been grown as a curiosity. It is expected that most gardens in Reykjavik will have small hothouses after the war, in order to utilize the waste water from the heating plant.

The Icelandic fishing banks are rated among the best in the world and the waters abound in every kind of fish. Icelanders are only one of the many nations fishing around Iceland, and their catch amounts to about 400,000 metric tons, or 900 million pounds.

Half of this gigantic catch is herring. In the beginning of July great areas of the sea suddenly turn red from tiny crabs that have come to life as suddenly as when a garden blossoms. Soon after, shoals of herring

*The quiet evening. Picture taken after ten o'clock at night*

become visible as dark patches on the immeasurable ocean, feeding on the crabs. Each shoal contains billions of herrings, and the sea is dotted with them. Often the pressure from beneath is such that the herrings in the topmost layers are lifted clear out of the water.

The fishing for cod takes place in winter and spring. Most of the fish is scooped up by steam trawlers dragging a great bag-like net, called a trawl, along the sea-bottom. Other fish, such as flatfish are caught in nets and on hooks by smaller vessels, which are mostly motor-boats built of oak. The trawl is suspected of destroying a great deal of life in the sea, and its use is therefore prohibited in Icelandic territorial waters, three miles from shore, both to foreign and our own fishermen. For years we

*Trawlers crowd the Icelandic fishing banks*

have been trying to reach an agreement with other fishing nations of the North Atlantic to outlaw the use of the trawl in Faxafloi, to keep it as a gigantic nursery area, where the young fish of little economic value in any case, are safeguarded from man.

Practically all the streams and lakes of Iceland are full of salmon and trout, both of which are excellent game fish. The world record for salmon fishing was made at a little river called Kjarrá.

The principal exports of Iceland are fish and fish products, for the products of agriculture are consumed in the country itself. During the war practically all the catch of fish went to Britain, where it helped considerably to relieve the shortage of protein foods, a fact that was greatly

*Distant mountains shelter the harbor of Reykjavik*

appreciated by the British Government. A considerable number of freezing plants have been erected, and it is expected that most of the catch will be sold quick-frozen after the war.

Iceland has long ranked among the five countries having the greatest foreign trade per capita. During the war it was at the top of the list, for foreign trade reached the sum of $500 to $600 per head of the population. The major portion of the trade is in the hands of individual merchants, but the cooperative movement is very strong in Iceland and takes care of the bulk of the needs of the farming population.

Most manufactured goods must be imported, but there is a considerable number of small factories, principally catering to the needs of the fishing industry, but also producing consumer goods such as clothes, soap, soft drinks, electric appliances, ceramics, etc.

Heavy traffic is transported mainly in steamers or motor-vessels along the coast, but most of the passenger traffic is now over land by motor cars or busses, with the arlines taking an increasing share. Owing to the scattered habitation road building is a rather heavy burden on the finances of Iceland. As the map at the end of this book shows, one could almost circle Iceland by motor-car in 1935, for great stress was laid on extending the road net to reach as many people as possible, and on making available cheap motor transport, even if it was only for the summer months. The step from horse transport to motor transport has meant a great stride forward in inland communication, breaking down the isolation of the individual farms.

We are expecting a similar stride forward when airplanes fly regularly between Iceland and the neighboring countries, in breaking down the isolation of Iceland. A few Icelandic companies expect to operate routes to Britain and to Scandinavia, but even apart from these, a considerable traffic is expected to go over Iceland in the future, since that is the shortest way to Scandinavia and Russia from America. It has the additional advantage that any storms there rarely, if ever, reach the height of 3000 feet, so that aircraft flying above that height are assured of constantly calm weather.

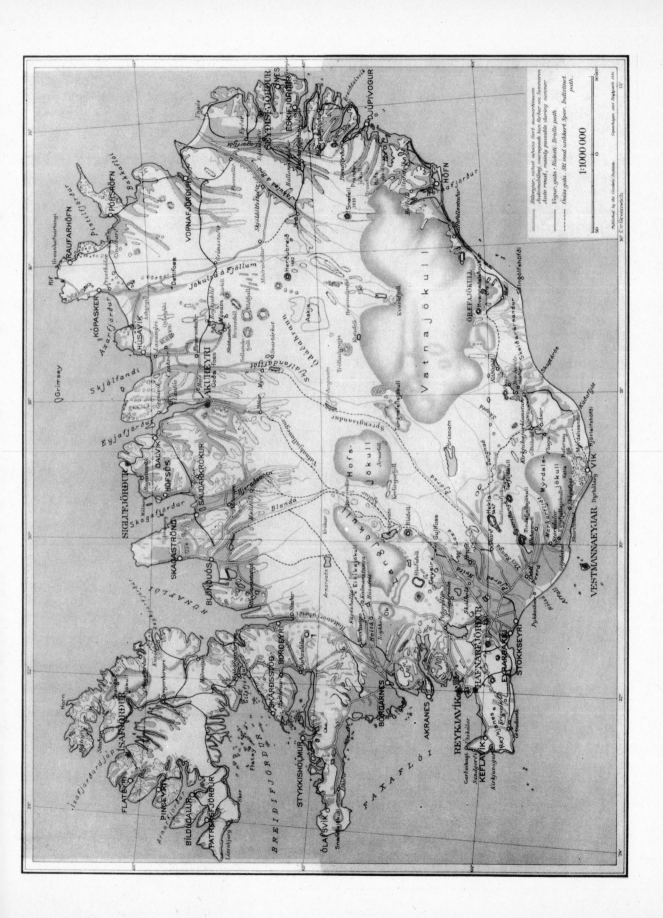

# LITERATURE

Readers are referred to the Catalogue of the Icelandic Collection of the Cornell University Library by Professor Halldor Hermannsson, published in 1914, with addenda in 1927 and 1943, for information on any special questions.

Here there are therefore only listed a few of the books available in English. Travel books are however omitted, because due to the rapid progress and changes in Iceland in this century only the most recent of these have any but historical interest.

Arason, S.: Smoky Bay, New York 1942

Beck, R.: Icelandic Lyrics, originals and translations, Reykjavik 1930

Beck, R.: Icelandic Poems and Stories, Princeton 1943

Blanchan, N.: The Bird Book, New York 1939

Bruun, D.: Iceland. Routes over the Highlands, Copenhagen 1907

Bryce, J. Lord: Memoirs of Travel, London 1923

Collingwood, W. G. and Jón Stefansson: A Pilgrimage to the Saga Steads of Iceland, Ulverston 1899

Craigie, W. A.: The Icelandic Sagas, Cambridge 1913

Einarsson, S.: Icelandic, Baltimore 1945

Gjerset, K.: History of Iceland, New York 1924

Hachisuka, M.: A Handbook of the Birds of Iceland, London 1927

Hermannsson, H.: The Problem of Wineland, Ithaca 1936

Hermannsson, H.: Icelandic Illuminated Manuscripts of the Middle Ages, Copenhagen 1935

Hermannsson, H.: Icelandic Authors of To-day, Ithaca 1913

Huntington, E.: The Character of Races, New York 1924

Johnson, S.: Pioneers of Freedom. An account of the Icelanders and the Icelandic Free State 874-1262, Boston 1930

Jonsson, S.: A Primer of Modern Icelandic, Oxford 1927

Jonsson, V.: Health in Iceland, Reykjavik, 1940

Kirkconnell, W.: The North American Book of Icelandic Verse, New York 1930

Kolderup-Rosenvinge, L. and E. Warming: The Botany of Iceland, London 1912 ff

Ostenfeld, C. H., and J. Grontved: The Flora of Iceland and the Faroes, Copenhagen 1934

Saemundsson, B.: Synopsis of the Fishes of Iceland, Reykjavik 1927

Stefansson, S.: Iceland, Handbook for Tourists, Reykjavik 1930

Stefansson, V.: Iceland. The First American Republic, New York 1939

Stefansson, V.: Ultima Thule, New York 1940

Steindorsson, S.: Contributions to the Plant Geography and Flora of Iceland, Reykjavik, 1935-37

Thordarson, B.: Iceland Past and Present, London 1941

Thordarson, M.: The Althing. Iceland's Thousand Year Old Parliament 930-1930, Reykjavik 1930

Thordarson, M.: The Vinland Voyages, New York 1930

Thorkellsson, T.: The Hot Springs in Iceland, Copenhagen 1910

Thoroddsen, T.: An Account of the Physical Geography of Iceland, Copenhagen 1914

Thorsteinsson, T. (Editor): Iceland 1936, Reykjavik 1936

Zoega, G. T.: English-Icelandic Dictionary, Reykjavik 1932

Zoega, G. T.: Icelandic-English Dictionary, Reykjavik 1922